Luke

Chapter-by-Chapter Bible Studies for Small Groups

By Barry L. Davis, D.Min., Ph.D.

Copyright©2023 Barry L. Davis

For More Chapter-By-Chapter Study Guides

Visit: <u>StudyChapterByChapter.com</u>

GodSpeed Publishing

2

Table of Contents

Introduction 5

Introduction to the Gospel of Luke 9

Fulfilled Prophecy in the Gospel of Luke 11

Additional Resources for Studying the Gospel of Luke 15

Luke Chapter 1 17

Luke Chapter 2 21

Luke Chapter 3 25

Luke Chapter 4 27

Luke Chapter 5 31

Luke Chapter 6 35

Luke Chapter 7 39

Luke Chapter 8 43

Luke Chapter 9 47

Luke Chapter 10 51

Luke Chapter 11 53

Luke Chapter 12 57

Luke Chapter 13 61

Luke Chapter 14 65

Luke Chapter 15 69

Luke Chapter 16 73

Luke Chapter 17 75

Luke Chapter 18 79

Luke Chapter 19 83

Luke Chapter 20 87

Luke Chapter 21 91

Luke Chapter 22 95

Luke Chapter 23 99

Luke Chapter 24 103

Conclusion 107

Introduction

Welcome to the Gospel of Luke Chapter-by-Chapter Bible study for small groups. This study guide is designed to help you dive deep into the life and teachings of Jesus Christ as recorded by Luke, one of the four evangelists. The Gospel of Luke is a treasure trove of insight and inspiration, offering a unique perspective on the life of Jesus, His ministry, and His impact on the world. As you journey through this study guide, our hope is that you will grow in your understanding of Jesus and His message, and that your faith will be strengthened and enriched.

The Gospel of Luke is the third of the four canonical gospels, and it is the longest of the synoptic gospels (Matthew, Mark, and Luke). Luke is known for its detailed and comprehensive account of Jesus' life, providing a historical and chronological perspective on His ministry. Some of the key themes and highlights of this gospel include the emphasis on Jesus' compassion for the poor and marginalized, His teachings on prayer and the Holy Spirit, and His focus on forgiveness and salvation.

Luke is unique in that it contains several parables and stories not found in the other gospels, such as the parable of the Good Samaritan, the parable of the Prodigal Son, and the story of the two disciples on the road to Emmaus. Through these stories, Luke highlights the importance of love, mercy, and the power of the gospel to transform lives.

For the best experience, we recommend that you read the corresponding chapter in the Gospel of Luke before diving into the study guide. This will help you become familiar with the content and context of the chapter, and it will allow you to engage with the questions and commentary more effectively. Whether you are studying alone or with a group, be sure to take the time to pray and ask the Holy Spirit to guide you in your study and open your heart to the truth of God's Word.

For small group studies, the Gospel of Luke presents numerous opportunities for rich discussion and fellowship. As you work through the study guide together, consider the following tips for fostering a fruitful and engaging group experience:

1. **Set the tone:** Create a welcoming and comfortable atmosphere where participants feel free to share their thoughts, ask questions, and engage in honest conversations about the text.

2. **Encourage participation:** Invite everyone in the group to contribute their insights and reflections. Ensure that no one person dominates the discussion and that all voices are heard.

3. **Stay focused:** Keep the conversation centered on the Scripture passage and the questions provided in the study guide. While it's natural for discussions to occasionally veer off course, gently redirect the group back to the main topic.

4. **Be sensitive to differing perspectives:** Recognize that group members may have different levels of familiarity with the Bible, various theological backgrounds, and diverse life experiences. Approach these differences with humility and grace, seeking to learn from one another and grow together in understanding.

5. **Pray together:** Begin and end each small group session with prayer, inviting the Holy Spirit to guide your study and asking for God's wisdom and discernment as you explore His Word.

6. **Provide accountability and support:** Encourage group members to share prayer requests and personal applications

from the study. Offer support, encouragement, and accountability as you journey together in your walk with Christ.

In conclusion, this Gospel of Luke Chapter-by-Chapter Bible Study Guide offers a rich resource for deepening your understanding of Jesus' life, teachings, and divine nature. Whether you are studying individually or in a small group setting, commit to engaging with the text prayerfully and thoughtfully, seeking to grow in your relationship with God and one another. May the Holy Spirit guide you as you explore the profound truths of the Gospel of John and experience the transformative power of God's Word in your life.

May God bless you as you dive into His Word and mine the deep riches it offers!

In Christ,

Barry L. Davis

Introduction to the Gospel of Luke

Background:

The Gospel of Luke is the third of the four Gospels in the New Testament, which recount the life, teachings, death, and resurrection of Jesus Christ. Luke's Gospel is particularly unique in its focus on the compassion, mercy, and love of Jesus for all people, especially the marginalized and outcasts of society. It also highlights the role of women and the importance of prayer. For those who know little to nothing about the book, this article will provide a detailed background on the Gospel of Luke to help you better understand its origins, purpose, and significance.

Authorship and Date:

Traditionally, the Gospel of Luke is attributed to Luke, a physician and companion of the apostle Paul. Although the Gospel itself is anonymous, early Christian tradition and writings, such as those of Irenaeus and Clement of Alexandria, affirm Luke's authorship. Luke is believed to have been a Gentile, making him the only non-Jewish author of a New Testament book. The Gospel of Luke is thought to have been written between AD 60 and 80, possibly around the same time as the Gospel of Matthew and after the Gospel of Mark.

Sources and Audience:

Luke explicitly states his intention to provide an "orderly account" of the events of Jesus' life, drawing from eyewitnesses and earlier written sources (Luke 1:1-4). It is widely believed that Luke used the Gospel of Mark as one of his primary sources, as well as a hypothetical source known as "Q" (from the German word "Quelle," meaning "source"), which is thought to be a collection of Jesus' sayings that was also used by the author of Matthew. Additionally,

Luke includes unique material not found in the other Gospels, often referred to as "L" (for Luke).

Purpose:

The intended audience of the Gospel of Luke is generally believed to be Gentile Christians, with a focus on instructing and edifying both new and established believers. The Gospel is dedicated to a certain "Theophilus" (Luke 1:3), which means "friend of God" or "lover of God" in Greek. This name may refer to a specific individual or may serve as a symbolic reference to any genuine seeker of truth.

Key Themes: Some of the key themes in the Gospel of Luke include:

- **Jesus' compassion and concern for the marginalized:** Luke emphasizes Jesus' love and care for those who were often neglected or rejected by society, such as tax collectors, sinners, women, the poor, and the sick.
- **The universality of salvation:** Luke underscores the message that the good news of salvation through Jesus is for everyone, regardless of their social status, nationality, or background.
- **The role of the Holy Spirit:** The Gospel of Luke highlights the work of the Holy Spirit in the life and ministry of Jesus, as well as in the lives of His followers.
- **The importance of prayer:** Luke frequently mentions Jesus' own practice of prayer and includes several parables and teachings on the subject.

Fulfilled Prophecy in the Gospel of Luke

One of the key aspects of the Gospel of Luke that sets it apart from the other Gospels is its emphasis on fulfilled prophecy. Luke, a physician and historian, carefully documents the fulfillment of numerous Old Testament prophecies in the life and ministry of Jesus Christ. This focus on fulfilled prophecy not only demonstrates the divine authority of Jesus but also underscores the reliability and trustworthiness of Scripture. In this article, we will explore some of the most significant instances of fulfilled prophecy in the Gospel of Luke and consider their implications for our faith.

1. The Birth of John the Baptist and Jesus (Luke 1-2)

The Gospel of Luke begins with the announcement of the birth of John the Baptist, the forerunner of Jesus, who is prophesied in Malachi 3:1 and Isaiah 40:3. Both prophecies speak of a messenger who will prepare the way for the Lord. In Luke 1:17, the angel Gabriel tells Zechariah, John's father, that John will fulfill this role by turning the hearts of the people back to God, preparing them for the coming of the Messiah.

The birth of Jesus is another significant fulfillment of prophecy in Luke's Gospel. The angel Gabriel appears to Mary and reveals that she will conceive a child by the Holy Spirit, fulfilling the prophecy in Isaiah 7:14, which states that a virgin will give birth to a son called Immanuel, meaning "God with us." The birth of Jesus in Bethlehem also fulfills the prophecy in Micah 5:2 that the Messiah would be born in this small town.

2. Jesus' Ministry in Nazareth (Luke 4:16-21)

In Luke 4, Jesus returns to his hometown of Nazareth and reads from the scroll of Isaiah in the synagogue. He reads from Isaiah 61:1-2, which speaks of the anointed one who will bring good news to the poor, freedom for prisoners, recovery of sight for the blind, and the year of the Lord's favor. After reading the passage, Jesus declares, "Today this scripture is fulfilled in your hearing" (Luke 4:21). In doing so, Jesus claims to be the fulfillment of this prophecy, announcing the beginning of His ministry and His divine mission to bring salvation to the world.

3. The Triumphal Entry (Luke 19:28-44)

As Jesus enters Jerusalem before His crucifixion, Luke records the fulfillment of Zechariah 9:9, which prophesies the coming of a king riding on a colt, the foal of a donkey. The people welcome Jesus, proclaiming Him as the Messiah, and laying down their cloaks and palm branches in His path. However, Jesus weeps over Jerusalem, knowing that the people have failed to recognize the time of God's visitation and that the city will eventually be destroyed as a consequence (Luke 19:41-44).

4. Jesus' Death and Resurrection (Luke 22-24)

The Gospel of Luke also highlights the fulfillment of prophecy in Jesus' death and resurrection. For example, Jesus' betrayal by Judas for thirty pieces of silver fulfills the prophecy in Zechariah 11:12-13. The mocking and abuse Jesus endures during His trial and crucifixion fulfill the prophecies in Isaiah 50:6 and Psalm 22. Furthermore, Jesus' resurrection from the dead fulfills the promise of the suffering servant in Isaiah 53, who will see the light of life and be vindicated by God.

The Gospel of Luke's emphasis on fulfilled prophecy demonstrates the divine nature of Jesus' life and ministry, as well as the reliability of Scripture. For believers today, these fulfilled prophecies serve as a powerful reminder of the truth of the Christian faith and the trustworthiness of God's promises. As we study the Gospel of Luke,

12

we can be encouraged by the fact that Jesus is indeed the long-awaited Messiah, the fulfillment of centuries of prophetic anticipation.

Additionally, the prophecies fulfilled in the Gospel of Luke provide a solid foundation for our faith and strengthen our confidence in the Bible as the inspired Word of God. They remind us that God is in control, orchestrating events throughout history to fulfill His purposes and bring about the salvation of humanity.

As we continue to study the Scriptures, we can trust that God's promises will be fulfilled, just as they were in the life of Jesus. This assurance gives us hope in times of uncertainty and challenges us to be faithful witnesses to the gospel, knowing that God's plan of redemption is unfolding according to His perfect will and timing.

In conclusion, the fulfilled prophecies in the Gospel of Luke serve as a testament to the divine authority of Jesus and the trustworthiness of Scripture. As we engage in personal or small group Bible studies, let us be mindful of these fulfilled prophecies, allowing them to deepen our understanding of the Gospel message and strengthen our faith in the God who keeps His promises.

Additional Resources for Studying the Gospel of Luke

Here is a list of great reference sources for those studying the Gospel of Luke. These resources include commentaries, scholarly works, and introductory texts that can provide valuable insights and perspectives on the themes, historical context, and theological significance of Luke's Gospel.

1. **Commentaries:**

   - The Gospel of Luke: A Commentary on the Greek Text (New International Greek Testament Commentary) by I. Howard Marshall

   - Luke: An Introduction and Commentary (Tyndale New Testament Commentaries) by Leon Morris

   - The Gospel According to Luke (Pillar New Testament Commentary) by James R. Edwards

   - The Gospel According to Luke (New American Commentary) by Robert H. Stein e. Luke (Expositor's Bible Commentary) by Walter L. Liefeld

2. **Scholarly works and introductory texts:**

   - Luke: Historian and Theologian by I. Howard Marshall

   - Prodigal Christianity: An Interpretation of the Parables of Jesus in Luke's Gospel by David E. Garland

   - The Theology of the Gospel of Luke by Joel B. Green

   - A Theology of Luke and Acts: God's Promised Program, Realized for All Nations (Biblical Theology of the New Testament) by Darrell L. Bock

3. **Online resources:**

- Bible Gateway (www.biblegateway.com) - Offers multiple translations, commentaries, and study resources.

- Blue Letter Bible (www.blueletterbible.org) - Provides access to commentaries, dictionaries, and cross-references.

- Bible Hub (www.biblehub.com) - Offers commentaries, lexicons, dictionaries, and other study tools.

- Bible.org (www.bible.org) - Provides articles, study resources, and commentaries by various scholars.

4. **Bible dictionaries and encyclopedias:**

- The IVP Bible Background Commentary: New Testament by Craig S. Keener

- Dictionary of Jesus and the Gospels (IVP Bible Dictionary) edited by Joel B. Green, Scot McKnight, and I. Howard Marshall

- The New Bible Dictionary (3rd Edition) edited by I. Howard Marshall, A.R. Millard, J.I. Packer, and D.J. Wiseman d. Zondervan Illustrated Bible Backgrounds Commentary: Matthew, Mark, Luke edited by Clinton E. Arnold

These resources can help deepen your understanding of the Gospel of Luke, providing valuable insights into the text, historical context, and theological themes. As you study, approach Scripture prayerfully and humbly, allowing the Holy Spirit to guide your understanding and application of God's Word.

Luke Chapter 1

Introduction:

- Summary: The Gospel of Luke begins with a prologue, stating the author's intention to provide an orderly account of the events concerning Jesus. The narrative starts with the miraculous conception of John the Baptist to the elderly and previously barren Elizabeth and her husband, Zechariah, a priest. The angel Gabriel appears to Mary, a young woman in Nazareth, announcing that she will conceive Jesus through the Holy Spirit. Mary visits Elizabeth, and they rejoice together. Mary praises God in the Magnificat, a song of praise. John the Baptist is born, and Zechariah, filled with the Holy Spirit, prophesies about his son's future ministry and the coming of the Messiah.

- Background: Luke's Gospel is written with a focus on providing an orderly and accurate account, drawing on various sources and eyewitnesses. The birth narratives of John the Baptist and Jesus emphasize God's intervention in history and the fulfillment of Old Testament prophecies.

- Parallel references: The birth narratives of John the Baptist and Jesus are unique to the Gospels of Luke and Matthew. The angel's announcement to Mary is found only in Luke, while the visit of the Magi and the flight to Egypt are found only in Matthew (Matthew 1-2).

1. Luke's Purpose in Writing (Luke 1:1-4):

- Discuss the author's intention in composing his Gospel account, focusing on his aim to provide an orderly and accurate record of the life and teachings of Jesus.

- Reflect on the importance of reliable testimony and historical accounts in building and maintaining faith. How can Luke's Gospel contribute to our confidence in the truth of Christianity?

2. **Gabriel Foretells John the Baptist's Birth (Luke 1:5-25):**

- Discuss the appearance of the angel Gabriel to Zechariah and the announcement of John the Baptist's birth. What role is John prophesied to play in God's plan?

- Reflect on Zechariah's initial disbelief and the consequences he experiences as a result. How does this story emphasize the importance of faith and trust in God's promises?

3. **Gabriel Foretells Jesus' Birth (Luke 1:26-38):**

- Examine the angel Gabriel's announcement to Mary about the miraculous conception and birth of Jesus. What key attributes and roles are attributed to Jesus in this passage?

- Consider Mary's humble response and willingness to be used by God. What can we learn from her example of faith and submission to God's will?

4. **Mary Visits Elizabeth (Luke 1:39-45):**

- Discuss the encounter between Mary and Elizabeth, focusing on Elizabeth's prophetic blessing and recognition of Jesus' divine nature. How does this meeting confirm and strengthen both women's faith?

- Reflect on the role of the Holy Spirit in this encounter. How does the Holy Spirit's presence in the lives of Mary, Elizabeth, and their unborn children emphasize the divine nature of these events?

5. **Mary's Song of Praise (Luke 1:46-56):**

- Analyze Mary's song of praise, also known as the Magnificat, and its themes of God's faithfulness, mercy, and justice. How do these themes resonate throughout salvation history?

- Consider the personal and communal implications of Mary's song. How can we apply the principles of her praise to our own lives and relationships with God and others?

6. The Birth of John the Baptist (Luke 1:57-80):

- Discuss the circumstances surrounding John the Baptist's birth, including the naming ceremony and Zechariah's regained ability to speak. How do these events confirm God's faithfulness and power?

- Examine Zechariah's prophecy concerning John's role as the forerunner of the Messiah. How does this prophecy set the stage for John's future ministry and the arrival of Jesus?

Reflection and Discussion:

- How does Luke Chapter 1 challenge and inspire you to trust in God's promises and recognize His divine plan at work in your life?
- What specific teachings or principles from Luke Chapter 1 can you apply to your own life to grow in your relationship with God and others?

Conclusion: As you reflect on Luke Chapter 1, seek to apply the insights and principles to your own faith and spiritual growth. Use this study guide to facilitate discussion, personal reflection, and spiritual growth as you delve into the themes of Luke's purpose in writing, angelic visitations, prophetic announcements, and faithful responses. May your engagement with Luke Chapter 1 deepen your understanding of God's Word and strengthen your relationship with God and others. As you explore these events and themes, consider how the examples of faith and trust in God's promises, displayed by Mary, Elizabeth, and Zechariah, can inspire and encourage you on your own spiritual journey.

Luke Chapter 2

Introduction:

- Summary: Jesus is born in Bethlehem during the time of a census ordered by Caesar Augustus. Angels announce His birth to shepherds, who visit the newborn Jesus. Jesus is presented at the Temple, where Simeon and Anna recognize Him as the Messiah and prophesy about His future. Jesus grows up in Nazareth, and at age 12, He visits the Temple in Jerusalem, astonishing the teachers with His wisdom.

- Background: The nativity story in Luke emphasizes the humble circumstances of Jesus' birth and His fulfillment of Old Testament prophecies. The stories of Simeon and Anna at the Temple highlight the recognition of Jesus as the promised Messiah from an early age.

- Parallel references: The nativity story is also found in Matthew (Matthew 1-2), but with different details, such as the visit of the Magi and the flight to Egypt. The story of Jesus at the Temple at age 12 is unique to the Gospel of Luke.

1. The Birth of Jesus in Bethlehem (Luke 2:1-7):

- Discuss the historical context and significance of the census that brought Mary and Joseph to Bethlehem. How does this event contribute to the fulfillment of prophecy regarding Jesus' birthplace?

- Reflect on the humble circumstances of Jesus' birth. What does this teach us about God's nature and the ways in which He works in our lives?

2. Shepherds and Angels (Luke 2:8-20):

- Examine the angelic announcement to the shepherds and their response. What does this event reveal about the importance of Jesus' birth and the role of the shepherds as witnesses?

- Consider the role of angels in this chapter. How do they serve to validate and communicate the significance of Jesus' birth?

3. **Jesus Presented at the Temple (Luke 2:21-40):**

- Analyze the events surrounding Jesus' presentation at the temple, including the prophecies of Simeon and Anna. What do these encounters reveal about Jesus' identity and mission?

- Reflect on the significance of the faithful responses of Simeon and Anna. What can we learn from their examples about recognizing and celebrating God's work in our lives?

4. **The Boy Jesus at the Temple (Luke 2:41-52):**

- Discuss the account of the young Jesus teaching and learning in the temple. What does this event reveal about Jesus' divine nature, His understanding of His identity, and His commitment to His mission?

- Reflect on the ways in which this event foreshadows Jesus' later ministry and interactions with religious leaders.

Reflection and Discussion:

- How does Luke Chapter 2 challenge and inspire you to recognize God's presence and work in your life, even in unexpected or humble circumstances?

- What specific teachings or principles from Luke Chapter 2 can you apply to your own life to grow in your relationship with God and others?

Conclusion: As you reflect on Luke Chapter 2, seek to apply the insights and principles to your own faith and spiritual growth. Use this study guide to facilitate discussion, personal reflection, and spiritual growth as you delve into the themes of Jesus' birth, the shepherds and angels, and Jesus at the temple. May your engagement with Luke Chapter 2 deepen your understanding of God's Word and strengthen your relationship with God and others.

Luke Chapter 3

Introduction:

- Summary: John the Baptist begins his ministry, preaching repentance and baptizing people in the Jordan River. John clarifies that he is not the Messiah but is preparing the way for Him. Jesus is baptized by John, and the Holy Spirit descends upon Him as a dove, with a voice from heaven proclaiming Him as God's Son. The chapter concludes with Jesus' genealogy, tracing His ancestry back to Adam.

- Background: John the Baptist's ministry serves as a precursor to Jesus' own ministry, emphasizing repentance and the coming of the Messiah. Jesus' baptism marks the beginning of His public ministry and affirms His identity as the Son of God.

- Parallel references: John's ministry and Jesus' baptism are found in all four Gospels (Matthew 3:1-17, Mark 1:1-11, and John 1:19-34). The genealogy in Luke differs from the one in Matthew (Matthew 1:1-17), which traces Jesus' lineage back to Abraham.

1. **John the Baptist's Ministry (Luke 3:1-20):**

- Discuss the historical context and significance of John the Baptist's ministry. How does John's message of repentance and baptism serve as a precursor to Jesus' ministry?

- Reflect on John's call for genuine repentance and justice. What implications does this have for our own spiritual lives and the ways we engage with the world?

2. **Jesus' Baptism (Luke 3:21-22):**

- Examine the account of Jesus' baptism by John, including the descent of the Holy Spirit and the voice from heaven. What does this event reveal about Jesus' identity and mission?

- Consider the significance of Jesus' baptism for His followers. How does Jesus' baptism serve as an example and foundation for Christian baptism?

3. **Jesus' Genealogy (Luke 3:23-38):**

- Analyze the genealogy of Jesus, noting the inclusion of various individuals and the connection to Adam. What does this genealogy teach us about Jesus' humanity, His divinity, and the fulfillment of prophecy?

- Reflect on the importance of understanding Jesus' genealogy in the context of salvation history. How does this help us appreciate the continuity and scope of God's plan?

Reflection and Discussion:

- How does Luke Chapter 3 challenge and inspire you to embrace repentance, seek justice, and recognize the significance of Jesus' baptism and genealogy?

- What specific teachings or principles from Luke Chapter 3 can you apply to your own life to grow in your relationship with God and others?

Conclusion: As you reflect on Luke Chapter 3, seek to apply the insights and principles to your own faith and spiritual growth. Use this study guide to facilitate discussion, personal reflection, and spiritual growth as you delve into the themes of John the Baptist's ministry, Jesus' baptism, and Jesus' genealogy. May your engagement with Luke Chapter 3 deepen your understanding of God's Word and strengthen your relationship with God and others.

Introduction:

- Summary: Jesus is led by the Holy Spirit into the wilderness, where He is tempted by the devil for 40 days. Jesus resists the temptations, using Scripture to counter Satan's attacks. He then begins His public ministry in Galilee, teaching in synagogues and gaining a following. In Nazareth, Jesus reads from the scroll of Isaiah and proclaims Himself as the fulfillment of the prophecy. The people reject Him, and He moves on to Capernaum, where He performs miracles and drives out demons. Jesus continues to teach and heal throughout Galilee, attracting large crowds.

- Background: The temptation of Jesus in the wilderness highlights His identity as the Son of God and His reliance on Scripture to resist temptation. The rejection in Nazareth foreshadows the wider rejection Jesus will face in His ministry. The miracles and exorcisms demonstrate Jesus' divine authority and power over evil.

- Parallel references: The temptation of Jesus is found in Matthew (Matthew 4:1-11) and Mark (Mark 1:12-13), with some variations in the order of the temptations. Jesus' ministry in Galilee and the rejection in Nazareth are also recounted in Matthew (Matthew 4:12-17, 13:53-58) and Mark (Mark 1:14-15, 6:1-6).

1. **Jesus' Temptation in the Wilderness (Luke 4:1-13):**

- Discuss the account of Jesus' temptation in the wilderness by the devil. How does Jesus use Scripture to counter each temptation, and what does this teach us about dealing with temptation in our own lives?

- Reflect on the significance of Jesus' victory over temptation. What does this reveal about His character, His mission, and His role as our example and Savior?

2. **Jesus' Rejection in Nazareth (Luke 4:14-30):**

- Examine Jesus' visit to the synagogue in Nazareth, where He reads from Isaiah and proclaims the fulfillment of prophecy. What is the significance of Jesus' statement, and how does it relate to His mission?

- Analyze the reaction of the people in the synagogue to Jesus' proclamation. Why do they reject Jesus, and what does this teach us about the nature of faith and unbelief?

3. **Jesus' Early Ministry in Galilee (Luke 4:31-44):**

- Discuss the various aspects of Jesus' early ministry in Galilee, including His teaching, healing, and exorcisms. What do these events reveal about Jesus' power, authority, and compassion?

- Reflect on the importance of Jesus' ministry in fulfilling prophecy and demonstrating the arrival of the kingdom of God. How does this deepen our understanding of Jesus' mission and message?

Reflection and Discussion:

- How does Luke Chapter 4 challenge and inspire you to rely on Scripture in facing temptation, recognize the fulfillment of prophecy, and appreciate the power and authority of Jesus' ministry?

- What specific teachings or principles from Luke Chapter 4 can you apply to your own life to grow in your relationship with God and others?

Conclusion: As you reflect on Luke Chapter 4, seek to apply the insights and principles to your own faith and spiritual growth. Use this study guide to facilitate discussion, personal reflection, and spiritual growth as you delve into the themes of Jesus' temptation, His rejection in Nazareth, and His early ministry in Galilee. May your engagement with Luke Chapter 4 deepen your understanding of God's Word and strengthen your relationship with God and others.

Luke Chapter 5

Introduction:

- Summary: Jesus calls His first disciples, Simon Peter, James, and John, after a miraculous catch of fish. He continues to teach and perform miracles, including healing a man with leprosy and a paralyzed man whose friends lower him through the roof of a house. Jesus calls Levi, a tax collector, to be His disciple, and He dines with Levi and other tax collectors, explaining that He has come to call sinners to repentance. Jesus teaches about fasting and introduces the concept of new wine in old wineskins.

- Background: The calling of the first disciples demonstrates Jesus' authority and His focus on building a community of followers. The miracles and teachings emphasize Jesus' compassion, divine authority, and His mission to call sinners to repentance.

- Parallel references: The calling of the first disciples is found in Matthew (Matthew 4:18-22) and Mark (Mark 1:16-20). The healing miracles and teachings on fasting are also found in Matthew (Matthew 8:1-4, 9:1-8, 9:14-17) and Mark (Mark 1:40-45, 2:1-12, 2:18-22).

1. **The Miraculous Catch of Fish (Luke 5:1-11):**

- Discuss the account of the miraculous catch of fish and the impact it had on Simon Peter and the other fishermen. What does this miracle teach us about Jesus' power, authority, and His ability to provide for our needs?

- Reflect on Jesus' call for Simon Peter, James, and John to become "fishers of men." What does this mean, and how does it relate to the mission of Jesus' followers today?

2. **Jesus Cleanses a Leper (Luke 5:12-16):**

- Examine the encounter between Jesus and the leper. Discuss the significance of Jesus' willingness to touch and heal the leper, despite the cultural and religious taboos associated with leprosy.

- Reflect on Jesus' instructions to the healed leper and the importance of following God's commands. Consider the impact this healing had on Jesus' ministry and the crowds seeking Him.

3. **Healing the Paralytic (Luke 5:17-26):**

- Analyze the story of the paralyzed man whose friends brought him to Jesus. Discuss the faith of the friends and their determination to bring the man to Jesus. What can we learn from their example?

- Focus on Jesus' response to the paralytic, examining His authority to forgive sins and His power to heal. What does this event reveal about Jesus' mission, identity, and divine authority?

4. **The Call of Levi (Luke 5:27-32):**

- Discuss the account of Jesus calling Levi (Matthew), a tax collector, and the subsequent dinner with other tax collectors and sinners. What do these events teach us about Jesus' inclusive ministry and the transformative power of His call?

- Reflect on the Pharisees' reaction to Jesus eating with tax collectors and sinners. Consider Jesus' response, "I have not come to call the righteous but sinners to repentance." How does this challenge our understanding of God's grace and our role in sharing it with others?

5. **The Parable of New Wine in Old Wineskins (Luke 5:33-39):**

- Examine the parable of new wine in old wineskins and the discussion of fasting. What does this parable teach us about the transformative nature of Jesus' ministry and the need for a new approach to faith?

- Reflect on the implications of this parable for our own spiritual lives. How can we ensure that we are receptive to the "new wine" of Jesus' teachings and the work of the Holy Spirit?

Reflection and Discussion:

- How does Luke Chapter 5 challenge and inspire you to recognize Jesus' authority, power, and transformative impact on people's lives?

- What specific teachings or principles from Luke Chapter 5 can you apply to your own life to grow in your relationship with God and others?

Conclusion: As you reflect on Luke Chapter 5, seek to apply the insights and principles to your own faith and spiritual growth. Use this study guide to facilitate discussion, personal reflection, and spiritual growth as you delve into the themes of the miraculous catch of fish, healing the paralytic, Jesus cleansing a leper, the call of Levi, and the parable of new wine in old wineskins. May your engagement with Luke Chapter 5 deepen your understanding of God's Word and strengthen your relationship with God and others.

Luke Chapter 6

Introduction:

- Summary: Jesus and His disciples pick grain on the Sabbath, leading to conflict with the Pharisees over Sabbath observance. Jesus heals a man with a withered hand on the Sabbath, further angering the Pharisees. Jesus chooses twelve of His followers to be apostles and delivers the Sermon on the Plain, which includes blessings and woes, teachings on love for enemies, judging others, and building one's life on a solid foundation.

- Background: The controversies over Sabbath observance highlight the tension between Jesus and the religious authorities. The Sermon on the Plain echoes the themes and teachings found in the Sermon on the Mount in Matthew, emphasizing the values of the Kingdom of God and the importance of living out one's faith.

- Parallel references: The Sabbath controversies are found in Matthew (Matthew 12:1-14) and Mark (Mark 2:23-28, 3:1-6). The Sermon on the Plain shares similarities with the Sermon on the Mount in Matthew (Matthew 5-7), though with some differences in content and setting.

1. Jesus, the Lord of the Sabbath (Luke 6:1-11):

- Discuss Jesus' actions on the Sabbath, focusing on His authority over the Sabbath and the reaction of the religious leaders. How do these events challenge traditional understandings of the Sabbath and demonstrate Jesus' divine authority?

- Reflect on the significance of Jesus' statement, "The Son of Man is Lord of the Sabbath." How does this deepen our understanding of Jesus' ministry and His role as the Messiah?

2. **The Selection of the Twelve Apostles (Luke 6:12-16):**

- Examine Jesus' selection of the twelve apostles, focusing on the importance of prayer in His decision-making process. What can we learn from Jesus' example of seeking God's guidance?

- Consider the significance of Jesus choosing a diverse group of individuals, including a former tax collector and a Zealot. What does this reveal about Jesus' inclusive ministry and His ability to transform lives?

3. **The Beatitudes and the Sermon on the Plain (Luke 6:17-26):**

- Analyze Jesus' teachings on the Beatitudes, focusing on the blessings promised to the poor, hungry, and persecuted. How do these teachings challenge conventional wisdom and offer hope to those who suffer?

- Reflect on the relevance of the Beatitudes to our own lives. How can we embody the values Jesus teaches in this passage?

4. **Love for Enemies and the Golden Rule (Luke 6:27-36):**

- Discuss Jesus' instruction to love enemies, focusing on the practical implications of this command. What does it mean to love our enemies, and how can we live out this teaching in our everyday lives?

- Examine the Golden Rule and its connection to the command to love enemies. How does this principle guide our interactions with others, even those who oppose or mistreat us?

5. Judging Others and Bearing Good Fruit (Luke 6:37-45):

- Explore Jesus' teachings on judging others and the importance of self-examination. How do these teachings challenge our natural tendencies to criticize and condemn others?

- Consider the metaphor of bearing good fruit. What does it mean to bear good fruit in our lives, and how can we cultivate a life that reflects the teachings of Jesus?

6. The Wise and Foolish Builders (Luke 6:46-49):

- Discuss the parable of the wise and foolish builders, focusing on the importance of building our lives on the solid foundation of Jesus' teachings. What does this parable teach us about the consequences of our choices and the importance of putting Jesus' teachings into practice?

- Reflect on your own life and consider how you can build on the solid foundation of Jesus' teachings. What practical steps can you take to ensure that your life is grounded in His words and teachings?

Reflection and Discussion:

- How does Luke Chapter 6 challenge and inspire you to recognize Jesus' authority, embrace His teachings on the Beatitudes, practice love for enemies, and build your life on a solid foundation?

- What specific teachings or principles from Luke Chapter 6 can you apply to your own life to grow in your relationship with God and others?

Conclusion: As you reflect on Luke Chapter 6, seek to apply the insights and principles to your own faith and spiritual growth. Use

this study guide to facilitate discussion, personal reflection, and spiritual growth as you delve into the themes of Jesus' authority over the Sabbath, the Beatitudes, love for enemies, and the parable of the wise and foolish builders. May your engagement with Luke Chapter 6 deepen your understanding of God's Word and strengthen your relationship with God and others.

Luke Chapter 7

Introduction:

- Summary: Jesus heals a centurion's servant from a distance, demonstrating His authority and the importance of faith. He raises a widow's son from the dead in the town of Nain, showing His compassion and power over death. John the Baptist, now in prison, sends his disciples to ask Jesus if He is the Messiah. Jesus responds by pointing to His miracles and teachings as evidence, and He praises John's role as a prophet. Jesus is anointed by a sinful woman at a Pharisee's house, and He forgives her sins, teaching about the relationship between love and forgiveness.

- Background: This chapter emphasizes Jesus' divine authority and power, as well as His compassion and mercy. The interaction with John the Baptist reaffirms Jesus' identity as the Messiah, and the anointing by the sinful woman illustrates the transformative power of Jesus' forgiveness.

- Parallel references: The healing of the centurion's servant is found in Matthew (Matthew 8:5-13), and the inquiry of John the Baptist is also found in Matthew (Matthew 11:2-6). The anointing by the sinful woman is similar to, but not identical with, the anointing stories in Matthew (Matthew 26:6-13), Mark (Mark 14:3-9), and John (John 12:1-8).

1. Jesus Heals a Centurion's Servant (Luke 7:1-10):

- Discuss the healing of the centurion's servant, focusing on the centurion's faith and humility. How does this event demonstrate Jesus' authority and the importance of faith?

- Reflect on the significance of the centurion's acknowledgement of Jesus' authority. What can we learn from his faith and approach to Jesus?

2. **Jesus Raises a Widow's Son (Luke 7:11-17):**

- Analyze the miracle of Jesus raising a widow's son from the dead. What does this event reveal about Jesus' compassion and power?

- Consider the impact of this miracle on the people who witnessed it. How does this event point to Jesus as the promised Messiah?

3. **Jesus and John the Baptist (Luke 7:18-35):**

- Examine the exchange between Jesus and John the Baptist's disciples, and Jesus' affirmation of John's role as the forerunner of the Messiah. What does this interaction teach us about Jesus' identity and mission?

- Reflect on Jesus' statements about John the Baptist, and the significance of John's role in preparing the way for Jesus. How does this help us understand the importance of recognizing Jesus as the Messiah?

4. **A Sinful Woman Anoints Jesus' Feet (Luke 7:36-50):**

- Discuss the encounter between Jesus and the sinful woman at Simon the Pharisee's house. What does this event reveal about Jesus' willingness to forgive and the importance of faith and repentance?

- Consider the contrast between the sinful woman's actions and Simon the Pharisee's attitude. What can we learn from this encounter about humility, forgiveness, and the transformative power of Jesus' love?

Reflection and Discussion:

- How does Luke Chapter 7 challenge and inspire you to have faith in Jesus' authority, embrace His compassion, and recognize the importance of repentance and forgiveness?

- What specific teachings or principles from Luke Chapter 7 can you apply to your own life to grow in your relationship with God and others?

Conclusion: As you reflect on Luke Chapter 7, seek to apply the insights and principles to your own faith and spiritual growth. Use this study guide to facilitate discussion, personal reflection, and spiritual growth as you delve into the themes of Jesus' healing ministry, the raising of a widow's son, the affirmation of John the Baptist, and the forgiveness of a sinful woman. May your engagement with Luke Chapter 7 deepen your understanding of God's Word and strengthen your relationship with God and others.

Luke Chapter 8

Introduction:

- Summary: Jesus travels and teaches with His disciples and several women who support His ministry. He tells the Parable of the Sower, emphasizing the importance of receptive hearts in receiving the Word of God. Jesus calms a storm, demonstrating His authority over nature, and He heals a demon-possessed man, showing His power over evil. Jesus also heals a woman who has been bleeding for 12 years and raises Jairus's daughter from the dead, illustrating His compassion and power to heal and give life.

- Background: The chapter highlights Jesus' teaching ministry and His divine authority through various miracles. The Parable of the Sower introduces the theme of the Kingdom of God and the importance of faith and receptiveness to God's Word.

- Parallel references: The Parable of the Sower, the calming of the storm, and the healing of the woman with the bleeding issue and Jairus's daughter are found in Matthew (Matthew 13:1-9, 8:23-27, 9:18-26) and Mark (Mark 4:1-9, 4:35-41, 5:21-43). The healing of the demon-possessed man is also found in Matthew (Matthew 8:28-34) and Mark (Mark 5:1-20).

1. **Women Who Supported Jesus and the Parable of the Sower (Luke 8:1-15):**

- Discuss the role of women who supported Jesus' ministry (Luke 8:1-3). What does this tell us about the inclusive nature of Jesus' ministry and the importance of all followers contributing to His work?

- Examine the Parable of the Sower, focusing on the different types of soil and their significance. What does this parable teach us about the receptiveness of our hearts to God's Word?

- Reflect on the importance of having a "good and noble heart" to receive and retain God's Word. How can we cultivate this kind of heart in our own lives?

2. **Jesus' Teachings on Light (Luke 8:16-21):**

- Explore Jesus' teachings on light and the importance of not hiding the light of God's Word (Luke 8:16-18). How do these teachings connect with the Parable of the Sower?

- Analyze Jesus' response to His mother and brothers in verses 19-21. What does this teach us about the importance of obedience and following the Word of God?

3. **Jesus Calms the Storm and Casts Out Demons (Luke 8:22-39):**

- Examine the miracle of Jesus calming the storm and casting out demons from a man. What do these events reveal about Jesus' authority over nature and spiritual forces?

- Consider the disciples' reaction to Jesus calming the storm and the people's reaction to the healed man. What can we learn from these responses about faith and recognizing Jesus' power?

4. **Healing of a Bleeding Woman and Raising of Jairus' Daughter (Luke 8:40-56):**

- Discuss the healing of the woman with a bleeding issue and the raising of Jairus' daughter. What do these miracles reveal about Jesus' power and compassion?

- Reflect on the role of faith in these healing stories. How do the individuals seeking healing demonstrate faith in Jesus, and what can we learn from their examples?

Reflection and Discussion:

- How does Luke Chapter 8 challenge and inspire you to cultivate a receptive heart, grow in faith, and practice obedience to God's Word?

- What specific teachings or principles from Luke Chapter 8 can you apply to your own life to grow in your relationship with God and others?

Conclusion: As you reflect on Luke Chapter 8, seek to apply the insights and principles to your own faith and spiritual growth. Use this study guide to facilitate discussion, personal reflection, and spiritual growth as you delve into the themes of parables, miracles, faith, and Jesus' teachings on light. May your engagement with Luke Chapter 8 deepen your understanding of God's Word and strengthen your relationship with God and others.

Luke Chapter 9

Introduction:

- Summary: Jesus sends out the twelve apostles to preach the Kingdom of God and heal the sick. Herod Antipas, the ruler of Galilee, hears about Jesus and wonders if John the Baptist has come back to life. Jesus miraculously feeds over 5,000 people with five loaves of bread and two fish, demonstrating His ability to provide abundantly. He asks His disciples who they think He is, and Peter confesses that Jesus is the Messiah. Jesus predicts His death and resurrection and teaches about the cost of discipleship. He is transfigured on a mountain, revealing His divine glory, and He later heals a boy with an unclean spirit. Jesus predicts His death and resurrection again and teaches about true greatness and the importance of welcoming children in His name.

- Background: This chapter continues to emphasize Jesus' divine authority and His role as the Messiah. The miracles, teachings, and transfiguration all serve to highlight Jesus' identity and mission.

- Parallel references: The sending of the twelve, the feeding of the 5,000, Peter's confession, Jesus' prediction of His death and resurrection, and the transfiguration are found in Matthew (Matthew 10:5-42, 14:13-21, 16:13-28, 17:1-13) and Mark (Mark 6:7-13, 6:30-44, 8:27-38, 9:2-13). The healing of the boy with an unclean spirit is also found in Matthew (Matthew 17:14-21) and Mark (Mark 9:14-29).

1. **Sending Out the Twelve and the Feeding of the Five Thousand (Luke 9:1-17):**

- Discuss the instructions and authority given to the twelve disciples as they are sent out to proclaim the kingdom of God and heal the sick. What does this event teach us about the role of the disciples in Jesus' ministry and their dependence on God?

- Examine the miracle of feeding the five thousand. What does this event reveal about Jesus' power and compassion? How does it challenge the disciples' faith and understanding of Jesus' identity?

2. **Peter's Confession of Christ and Jesus Predicts His Death (Luke 9:18-27):**

- Analyze Peter's confession of Jesus as the Christ and Jesus' response. What is the significance of this moment in Jesus' ministry?

- Reflect on Jesus' prediction of His death and the implications for His disciples. How does this teaching challenge their expectations of the Messiah?

3. **The Transfiguration (Luke 9:28-36):**

Explore the event of Jesus' transfiguration, focusing on the appearance of Moses and Elijah and the voice of God affirming Jesus' identity. What does this event teach us about Jesus' divine nature and His fulfillment of the Law and the Prophets?

Consider the disciples' reaction to the transfiguration. What can we learn from their experience about recognizing and responding to God's presence?

4. **Healing a Demon-Possessed Boy and Jesus Predicts His Death Again (Luke 9:37-45):**

- Discuss Jesus' healing of the demon-possessed boy and the disciples' inability to do so. What does this event reveal about the importance of faith and reliance on God's power?

- Reflect on Jesus' second prediction of His death. How do the disciples struggle to understand Jesus' mission and the implications for their own lives?

5. Teachings on Discipleship and True Greatness (Luke 9:46-62):

- Examine Jesus' teachings on true greatness, welcoming the little ones, and the cost of following Him. What do these teachings reveal about the nature of discipleship and the priorities of Jesus' kingdom?

- Consider the challenges and commitments that Jesus presents to those who want to follow Him. How can we apply these principles to our own lives as modern-day disciples?

Reflection and Discussion:

- How does Luke Chapter 9 challenge and inspire you to grow in faith, recognize Jesus' identity, and embrace the demands of discipleship?

- What specific teachings or principles from Luke Chapter 9 can you apply to your own life to grow in your relationship with God and others?

Conclusion: As you reflect on Luke Chapter 9, seek to apply the insights and principles to your own faith and spiritual growth. Use this study guide to facilitate discussion, personal reflection, and spiritual growth as you delve into the themes of sending out the twelve, Jesus' identity, the transfiguration, and teachings on discipleship. May your engagement with Luke Chapter 9 deepen your understanding of God's Word and strengthen your relationship with God and others.

Luke Chapter 10

Introduction:

- Summary: Jesus sends out 72 disciples to proclaim the Kingdom of God and heal the sick. They return rejoicing at their success, and Jesus praises God for revealing His truth to the humble. Jesus tells the Parable of the Good Samaritan in response to a question about who one's neighbor is, emphasizing the importance of love and compassion. Jesus visits the home of Mary and Martha, where Mary sits at Jesus' feet to listen to His teaching, highlighting the priority of spiritual nourishment.

- Background: This chapter focuses on the expansion of Jesus' ministry through the sending of the 72 disciples and His teachings on love, compassion, and spiritual priorities.

- Parallel references: The sending of the 72 disciples is unique to the Gospel of Luke. The Parable of the Good Samaritan is also unique to Luke. The story of Mary and Martha is found only in Luke as well.

1. **The Mission of the Seventy-Two (Luke 10:1-24):**

- Discuss Jesus' instructions and purpose for sending out the seventy-two disciples. How do these instructions emphasize the urgency and importance of their mission?

- Reflect on Jesus' words about the towns that reject the message. What does this teach us about the consequences of rejecting the gospel?

2. **The Parable of the Good Samaritan (Luke 10:25-37):**

51

- Examine the parable of the Good Samaritan in response to the question, "Who is my neighbor?" What does this parable teach about the nature of love and compassion?

- Discuss the actions of the priest, the Levite, and the Samaritan. How does Jesus challenge our understanding of who our neighbors are and what it means to be a neighbor?

3. **Mary and Martha (Luke 10:38-42):**

- Analyze the story of Mary and Martha, focusing on their different responses to Jesus' presence. What does this story teach us about the importance of prioritizing our relationship with Jesus and finding balance in our lives?

- Reflect on Jesus' words to Martha about choosing the "better part." How can we apply this lesson to our own lives as we seek to grow in our relationship with Jesus and serve others?

Reflection and Discussion:

- How does Luke Chapter 10 challenge and inspire you to embrace the urgency of sharing the gospel, practice neighborly love, and prioritize your relationship with Jesus?

- What specific teachings or principles from Luke Chapter 10 can you apply to your own life to grow in your relationship with God and others?

Conclusion: As you reflect on Luke Chapter 10, seek to apply the insights and principles to your own faith and spiritual growth. Use this study guide to facilitate discussion, personal reflection, and spiritual growth as you delve into the themes of the mission of the seventy-two, the parable of the Good Samaritan, and Mary and Martha. May your engagement with Luke Chapter 10 deepen your understanding of God's Word and strengthen your relationship with God and others.

Luke Chapter 11

Introduction:

- Summary: Jesus teaches His disciples to pray using the Lord's Prayer, emphasizing persistence in prayer and God's willingness to provide for His children. Jesus casts out a demon and is accused of using Satan's power to do so, but He refutes the accusation by asserting that a divided kingdom cannot stand. He teaches about the importance of spiritual light and criticizes the Pharisees and experts in the law for their hypocrisy and neglect of justice, mercy, and faithfulness.

- Background: This chapter contains teachings on prayer, spiritual warfare, and the danger of religious hypocrisy. The Lord's Prayer serves as a model for addressing God and seeking His provision and guidance.

- Parallel references: The Lord's Prayer is also found in Matthew (Matthew 6:9-13). The accusation against Jesus of casting out demons by Satan's power is found in Matthew (Matthew 12:22-37) and Mark (Mark 3:20-30). The criticisms of the Pharisees and experts in the law are similar to those in Matthew (Matthew 23).

1. Jesus Teaches on Prayer (Luke 11:1-13):

- Examine Jesus' instructions on prayer, focusing on the Lord's Prayer. What key elements can we learn from this model prayer to incorporate into our own prayer life?

- Discuss the parable of the persistent friend and Jesus' teachings on asking, seeking, and knocking. What does this passage teach us about persistence and faith in prayer?

2. Jesus and Beelzebul (Luke 11:14-28):

- Analyze Jesus' response to the accusation that He casts out demons by the power of Beelzebul. How does Jesus refute this claim and reveal the true source of His authority?

- Reflect on Jesus' statement about those who are not with Him being against Him. What does this teach us about the importance of aligning ourselves with Jesus and His mission?

3. The Sign of Jonah and the Judgment of the Pharisees (Luke 11:29-36):

- Discuss Jesus' reference to the sign of Jonah and His refusal to provide a sign for the unbelieving generation. How does this passage emphasize the importance of faith and spiritual discernment?

- Consider the parable of the lamp and its application to our lives. How can we ensure that we are filled with spiritual light and not darkness?

4. Woes Against the Pharisees and Experts in the Law (Luke 11:37-54):

- Examine the series of woes Jesus pronounces against the Pharisees and experts in the law. What common themes emerge from these rebukes, and what do they reveal about the hypocrisy of the religious leaders?

- Reflect on Jesus' warnings against the Pharisees and experts in the law. How can we guard against similar attitudes and behaviors in our own lives?

Reflection and Discussion:

- How does Luke Chapter 11 challenge and inspire you to develop a deeper prayer life, recognize Jesus' authority, and avoid hypocrisy in your spiritual journey?

- What specific teachings or principles from Luke Chapter 11 can you apply to your own life to grow in your relationship with God and others?

Conclusion: As you reflect on Luke Chapter 11, seek to apply the insights and principles to your own faith and spiritual growth. Use this study guide to facilitate discussion, personal reflection, and spiritual growth as you delve into the themes of prayer, casting out demons, and warnings against the Pharisees. May your engagement with Luke Chapter 11 deepen your understanding of God's Word and strengthen your relationship with God and others.

Luke Chapter 12

Introduction:

- Summary: Jesus warns against hypocrisy and teaches His followers not to fear persecution, as God values and cares for them. He tells the Parable of the Rich Fool, cautioning against greed and the pursuit of earthly possessions. Jesus encourages His disciples to seek the Kingdom of God and not worry about their material needs. He teaches about readiness for His return, using the Parable of the Faithful and Unfaithful Servants. Jesus speaks about division, judgment, and the need to discern the signs of the times and settle disputes.

- Background: This chapter contains teachings on spiritual priorities, trust in God, and the need for vigilance in anticipation of Jesus' return. The parables and teachings emphasize the values of the Kingdom of God and the importance of a faithful and discerning life.

- Parallel references: The Parable of the Rich Fool is unique to the Gospel of Luke. The teachings on trust in God and the Parable of the Faithful and Unfaithful Servants are found in Matthew (Matthew 6:25-34, 24:45-51).

1. Warnings Against Hypocrisy and Fear (Luke 12:1-12):

- Discuss Jesus' warning against the hypocrisy of the Pharisees and the encouragement not to fear those who can only harm the body. What lessons can we learn from this passage about the dangers of hypocrisy and the importance of fearing God?

- Reflect on Jesus' promise of the Holy Spirit's guidance when facing persecution. How does this assurance provide comfort and encouragement for believers?

2. **The Parable of the Rich Fool (Luke 12:13-21):**

- Analyze the Parable of the Rich Fool, focusing on the dangers of greed and the foolishness of relying on material wealth. What key principles can we draw from this parable to help us prioritize our spiritual lives over worldly pursuits?

- Consider the implications of this parable for our own lives. How can we guard against the temptations of greed and ensure that we are rich toward God?

3. **Do Not Worry; Trust in God's Provision (Luke 12:22-34):**

- Examine Jesus' teachings on worry and His encouragement to trust in God's provision. How do these teachings challenge our worldly perspectives and encourage reliance on God?

- Reflect on practical ways we can apply Jesus' teachings on worry and trust in our own lives. How can we cultivate a deeper sense of trust in God's care for us?

4. **Be Ready for the Lord's Return (Luke 12:35-48):**

- Discuss Jesus' teachings on the importance of being ready for His return, focusing on the parable of the servants waiting for their master's return. What does this passage teach us about the importance of vigilance and faithfulness in our Christian walk?

- Reflect on the parable of the wise and foolish managers. How can we apply the principles of this parable to our own lives to ensure that we are faithful stewards of what God has entrusted to us?

5. **Not Peace, but Division, and Interpreting the Times (Luke 12:49-59):**

- Examine Jesus' statement about bringing division rather than peace and the need to understand the signs of the times. How do these teachings challenge our expectations of Jesus' ministry and the role of believers in the world?

- Reflect on the importance of discerning the spiritual climate and being proactive in addressing issues in our own lives and the world around us. How can we apply these principles to better understand the times in which we live?

Reflection and Discussion:

- How does Luke Chapter 12 challenge and inspire you to guard against hypocrisy, prioritize your spiritual life, trust in God's provision, and be ready for the Lord's return?

- What specific teachings or principles from Luke Chapter 12 can you apply to your own life to grow in your relationship with God and others?

Conclusion: As you reflect on Luke Chapter 12, seek to apply the insights and principles to your own faith and spiritual growth. Use this study guide to facilitate discussion, personal reflection, and spiritual growth as you delve into the themes of warnings and encouragements, the Parable of the Rich Fool, and being ready for the Lord's return. May your engagement with Luke Chapter 12 deepen your understanding of God's Word and strengthen your relationship with God and others.

Luke Chapter 13

Introduction:

- Summary: Jesus teaches about the need for repentance and the urgency of turning to God, using the examples of the Galileans killed by Pilate and the Tower of Siloam incident. He heals a woman who has been crippled for 18 years on the Sabbath, leading to controversy with religious leaders. Jesus teaches about the nature of the Kingdom of God using the Parables of the Mustard Seed and the Yeast. He laments over Jerusalem and its rejection of prophets, including Himself.

- Background: This chapter emphasizes the need for repentance and the urgency of accepting Jesus' message. The healing on the Sabbath continues to highlight the tension between Jesus and the religious authorities. The parables illustrate the growth and transformative power of the Kingdom of God.

- Parallel references: The Parables of the Mustard Seed and the Yeast are found in Matthew (Matthew 13:31-33) and Mark (Mark 4:30-32). Jesus' lament over Jerusalem is also found in Matthew (Matthew 23:37-39).

1. The Call to Repentance (Luke 13:1-5):

- Discuss Jesus' response to the tragedies of the Galileans and the tower of Siloam. What is the central message of these passages, and how does it emphasize the importance of repentance in our lives?

- Reflect on the urgency of Jesus' call for repentance. What does this teach us about the nature of God's grace and the consequences of remaining unrepentant?

2. The Parable of the Barren Fig Tree (Luke 13:6-9):

- Analyze the parable of the barren fig tree, focusing on the importance of bearing fruit and the consequences of being unfruitful. What does this parable teach us about the expectations God has for His people?

- Consider the implications of this parable for our own spiritual lives. How can we bear fruit in our lives and respond to God's call for repentance and spiritual growth?

3. Healing on the Sabbath and Jesus' Response to Hypocrisy (Luke 13:10-17):

- Discuss the healing of the crippled woman on the Sabbath and Jesus' response to the synagogue leader. What do these events teach us about Jesus' priorities and the dangers of religious hypocrisy?

- Consider the importance of placing compassion and mercy above legalistic observance of religious rules. How can we apply this lesson to our own lives and faith practices?

4. Parables of the Mustard Seed and Yeast (Luke 13:18-21):

- Examine the parables of the mustard seed and the yeast, focusing on the nature and growth of God's kingdom. What do these parables reveal about the transformative power of faith and the potential for growth within God's kingdom?

- Reflect on the implications of these parables for our own spiritual lives. How can we participate in the growth of God's kingdom and allow our faith to flourish?

5. The Narrow Door and Jesus' Teaching on Salvation (Luke 13:22-30):

- Explore Jesus' teaching on the narrow door and the challenge of entering the kingdom of God. What does this teach us about the nature of salvation and the importance of striving to enter the kingdom?

- Reflect on the implications of Jesus' teaching for our own spiritual lives. How can we ensure that we are pursuing a genuine relationship with God and not relying on superficial connections?

6. Jesus' Lament Over Jerusalem (Luke 13:31-35):

- Analyze Jesus' lament over Jerusalem, focusing on His sorrow for the city and His longing to gather its people as a hen gathers her chicks. What does this reveal about Jesus' heart for the lost and the consequences of rejecting His message?

- Consider the implications of Jesus' lament for our own spiritual lives. How can we respond to Jesus' call for repentance and ensure that we do not miss the opportunity for salvation?

Reflection and Discussion:

- How does Luke Chapter 13 challenge and inspire you to embrace repentance, participate in the growth of God's kingdom, prioritize compassion and mercy, and respond to Jesus' call for salvation?

- What specific teachings or principles from Luke Chapter 13 can you apply to your own life to grow in your relationship with God and others?

Conclusion: As you reflect on Luke Chapter 13, seek to apply the insights and principles to your own faith and spiritual growth. Use this study guide to facilitate discussion, personal reflection, and spiritual growth as you delve into the themes of repentance, parables of the kingdom, healing on the Sabbath, and Jesus' lament over Jerusalem. May your engagement with Luke Chapter 13 deepen your understanding of God's Word and strengthen your relationship with God and others.

Luke Chapter 14

Introduction:

- Summary: Jesus heals a man with dropsy on the Sabbath at a Pharisee's house and teaches about humility and the importance of inviting the poor and marginalized to feasts. He tells the Parable of the Great Banquet, emphasizing the need to accept God's invitation and the consequences of rejecting it. Jesus teaches about the cost of discipleship and the importance of counting the cost before committing to follow Him. He uses the Parables of the Tower Builder and the Warring King to illustrate this point and concludes by teaching about the need to be salt that retains its flavor.

- Background: This chapter highlights Jesus' teachings on humility, generosity, the cost of discipleship, and the importance of maintaining one's spiritual integrity. The parables illustrate the consequences of rejecting God's invitation and the importance of being fully committed to following Jesus.

- Parallel references: The Parable of the Great Banquet is found in Matthew (Matthew 22:1-14), although in a slightly different context. The teachings on the cost of discipleship and the salt that retains its flavor are also found in Matthew (Matthew 10:37-39, 5:13) and Mark (Mark 9:50).

1. Healing on the Sabbath (Luke 14:1-6):

- Discuss Jesus' healing of the man with dropsy on the Sabbath and the reaction of the religious leaders. What does this event teach us about Jesus' priorities and the nature of God's kingdom?

- Reflect on the significance of Jesus healing on the Sabbath in relation to legalism and compassion. How can we ensure that our understanding of God's law is balanced with love and mercy?

2. Parable of the Wedding Feast and Humility (Luke 14:7-11):

- Examine Jesus' parable of the wedding feast and the lesson of humility. What does this parable reveal about the values of God's kingdom and how we should approach our relationships with others?

- Consider the statement, "For everyone who exalts himself will be humbled, and he who humbles himself will be exalted." How can we apply this principle to our own lives and grow in humility?

3. Parable of the Great Banquet (Luke 14:12-24):

- Discuss the parable of the great banquet, focusing on the invitation to the feast and the excuses offered by those who were initially invited. What does this parable teach us about the inclusiveness of God's kingdom and the priorities of those who follow Jesus?

- Reflect on the implications of this parable for our own spiritual lives. How can we ensure that we are receptive to God's invitation and prioritize His kingdom in our lives?

4. The Cost of Discipleship (Luke 14:25-35):

- Analyze Jesus' teaching on the cost of discipleship, including the need to put Jesus first, carry our cross, and count the cost. What do these teachings reveal about the demands and rewards of following Jesus?

- Consider the metaphors of the salt losing its saltiness and the unfinished tower. How do these images emphasize the importance of commitment and perseverance in our walk with Christ?

Reflection and Discussion:

- How does Luke Chapter 14 challenge and inspire you to prioritize God's kingdom, embrace humility, and count the cost of discipleship?

- What specific teachings or principles from Luke Chapter 14 can you apply to your own life to grow in your relationship with God and others?

Conclusion: As you reflect on Luke Chapter 14, seek to apply the insights and principles to your own faith and spiritual growth. Use this study guide to facilitate discussion, personal reflection, and spiritual growth as you delve into the themes of healing on the Sabbath, the parables of the wedding feast and the great banquet, and the cost of discipleship. May your engagement with Luke Chapter 14 deepen your understanding of God's Word and strengthen your relationship with God and others.

Luke Chapter 15

Introduction:

- Summary: Jesus tells three parables in response to the Pharisees' and scribes' grumbling about His association with sinners: the Parable of the Lost Sheep, the Parable of the Lost Coin, and the Parable of the Prodigal Son. These parables emphasize God's love for sinners, the joy in heaven over their repentance, and the importance of a forgiving and merciful attitude.

- Background: This chapter focuses on Jesus' teachings about God's love, mercy, and forgiveness, which stand in contrast to the judgmental attitudes of the religious leaders. The parables emphasize the value God places on each individual and the joy that comes from repentance and reconciliation.

- Parallel references: The Parable of the Lost Sheep is also found in Matthew (Matthew 18:12-14). The Parables of the Lost Coin and the Prodigal Son are unique to the Gospel of Luke.

1. Parable of the Lost Sheep (Luke 15:1-7):

- Discuss the parable of the lost sheep, focusing on the shepherd's determination to find the lost sheep and the rejoicing that follows. What does this parable teach us about God's love, His pursuit of the lost, and the value He places on each individual?

- Reflect on the statement, "I tell you that in the same way there will be more rejoicing in heaven over one sinner who repents than over ninety-nine righteous persons who do not need to repent." How does this reveal God's heart for those who are lost and the importance of repentance?

2. **Parable of the Lost Coin (Luke 15:8-10):**

- Examine the parable of the lost coin and the woman's diligent search for it. What does this parable reveal about God's desire to find and restore the lost?

- Consider the celebration that takes place when the lost coin is found. How does this parable emphasize the joy in heaven when someone repents and is restored to God?

3. **Parable of the Prodigal Son (Luke 15:11-32):**

- Analyze the parable of the prodigal son, focusing on the younger son's rebellion, repentance, and restoration. What does this parable teach us about the consequences of sin, the process of repentance, and the grace of God?

- Discuss the father's response to the prodigal son's return and the older son's reaction. What do these responses reveal about God's unconditional love and the importance of having a heart that celebrates the restoration of others?

Reflection and Discussion:

- How do the three parables in Luke Chapter 15 challenge and inspire you to recognize God's love and forgiveness, the value He places on each person, and the joy of restoration?

- What specific teachings or principles from Luke Chapter 15 can you apply to your own life to grow in your understanding of God's love and grace and to reach out to those who are lost?

Conclusion: As you reflect on Luke Chapter 15, seek to apply the insights and principles to your own faith and spiritual growth. Use

this study guide to facilitate discussion, personal reflection, and spiritual growth as you delve into the themes of God's love, forgiveness, and the joy of restoration. May your engagement with Luke Chapter 15 deepen your understanding of God's Word and strengthen your relationship with God and others.

Luke Chapter 16

Introduction:

- Summary: Jesus tells the Parable of the Shrewd Manager, encouraging His followers to be wise in their use of worldly resources for eternal purposes. He teaches about faithfulness in handling wealth and the impossibility of serving both God and money. Jesus tells the story of the Rich Man and Lazarus, emphasizing the importance of heeding God's Word and the consequences of ignoring the needs of others.

- Background: This chapter contains teachings on wealth, stewardship, and the consequences of one's choices in life. The parables and teachings stress the importance of using resources wisely and prioritizing eternal values over worldly wealth.

- Parallel references: The Parable of the Shrewd Manager is unique to the Gospel of Luke. The teachings about faithfulness in handling wealth and the impossibility of serving both God and money are found in Matthew (Matthew 6:24). The story of the Rich Man and Lazarus is also unique to Luke.

1. Parable of the Shrewd Manager (Luke 16:1-15):

- Discuss the parable of the shrewd manager, focusing on his actions and the master's response. What does this parable teach us about stewardship, faithfulness, and the use of our earthly resources?

- Reflect on Jesus' statement, "Whoever can be trusted with very little can also be trusted with much, and whoever is dishonest with very little will also be dishonest with much."

How does this principle apply to our lives, and what can we learn from it?

2. **The Rich Man and Lazarus (Luke 16:19-31):**

- Examine the parable of the rich man and Lazarus, focusing on the contrast between their earthly lives and their eternal destinies. What does this parable teach us about the consequences of our actions and the importance of compassion and generosity?

- Consider the rich man's plea for his brothers and Abraham's response. What does this exchange reveal about the sufficiency of God's Word and the importance of heeding its teachings in our lives?

Reflection and Discussion:

- How do the two parables in Luke Chapter 16 challenge and inspire you to be faithful stewards of the resources God has entrusted to you and to demonstrate compassion and generosity towards others?

- What specific teachings or principles from Luke Chapter 16 can you apply to your own life to grow in your relationship with God and your understanding of stewardship, faithfulness, and compassion?

Conclusion: As you reflect on Luke Chapter 16, seek to apply the insights and principles to your own faith and spiritual growth. Use this study guide to facilitate discussion, personal reflection, and spiritual growth as you delve into the themes of stewardship, faithfulness, and the use of earthly resources. May your engagement with Luke Chapter 16 deepen your understanding of God's Word and strengthen your relationship with God and others.

Luke Chapter 17

Introduction:

- Summary: Jesus teaches about the inevitability of stumbling blocks and the importance of forgiveness and faith. He heals ten lepers, but only one, a Samaritan, returns to thank Him, illustrating the importance of gratitude and the universality of God's mercy. Jesus teaches about the nature of the Kingdom of God and the suddenness of His return, using the examples of Noah and Lot to emphasize the need for readiness and vigilance.

- Background: This chapter highlights Jesus' teachings on forgiveness, faith, gratitude, and preparedness for His return. The healing of the ten lepers demonstrates God's mercy and the need for genuine gratitude in response to His blessings.

- Parallel references: The teachings on stumbling blocks, forgiveness, and faith are found in Matthew (Matthew 18:6-7, 18:21-22). The teachings on the suddenness of Jesus' return and the examples of Noah and Lot are also found in Matthew (Matthew 24:37-39).

1. Teachings on Faith and Forgiveness (Luke 17:1-10):

- Discuss Jesus' teaching on the importance of avoiding causing others to stumble and the necessity of forgiving those who have wronged us. How do these teachings challenge and inspire us to be more mindful of our actions and more gracious towards others?

- Reflect on Jesus' statement about faith as small as a mustard seed. What does this teach us about the power and potential of even the smallest amount of faith in our lives?

2. The Healing of the Ten Lepers (Luke 17:11-19):

- Examine the story of the ten lepers who were healed by Jesus, focusing on the actions of the one who returned to give thanks. What does this story teach us about gratitude and the importance of recognizing and appreciating God's blessings in our lives?

- Consider the significance of the fact that the one who returned to give thanks was a foreigner. What might this detail reveal about the inclusivity and reach of Jesus' ministry and the Kingdom of God?

3. The Coming of the Kingdom of God (Luke 17:20-37):

- Discuss Jesus' teachings about the coming of the Kingdom of God, focusing on the suddenness and unpredictability of its arrival. How do these teachings call us to be vigilant and prepared in our faith and actions?

- Reflect on the examples Jesus uses to describe the days of the coming of the Kingdom, such as the days of Noah and Lot. What can we learn from these examples about the importance of not being caught up in worldly concerns when the Kingdom comes?

Reflection and Discussion:

- How does Luke Chapter 17 challenge and inspire you to grow in faith, forgiveness, gratitude, and vigilance in anticipation of the coming of the Kingdom of God?

- What specific teachings or principles from Luke Chapter 17 can you apply to your own life to grow in your relationship with God and others?

Conclusion: As you reflect on Luke Chapter 17, seek to apply the insights and principles to your own faith and spiritual growth. Use this study guide to facilitate discussion, personal reflection, and spiritual growth as you delve into the themes of faith, forgiveness, gratitude, and the coming of the Kingdom of God. May your engagement with Luke Chapter 17 deepen your understanding of God's Word and strengthen your relationship with God and others.

Luke Chapter 18

Introduction:

- Summary: Jesus tells the Parable of the Persistent Widow, emphasizing the importance of persistent prayer and faith. He also tells the Parable of the Pharisee and the Tax Collector, highlighting the need for humility and genuine repentance. Jesus blesses the little children, teaching about the importance of receiving the Kingdom of God with childlike faith. He encounters the Rich Young Ruler, stressing the need for complete devotion to God and the difficulty of wealth in entering the Kingdom of God. Jesus predicts His death and resurrection for the third time, and He heals a blind beggar near Jericho, demonstrating His compassion and power.

- Background: This chapter contains teachings on prayer, faith, humility, and the challenges of wealth in following Jesus. The parables and encounters emphasize the importance of genuine devotion to God and reliance on His mercy and grace.

- Parallel references: The Parable of the Persistent Widow and the Parable of the Pharisee and the Tax Collector are unique to the Gospel of Luke. The blessing of the little children, the encounter with the Rich Young Ruler, and the healing of the blind beggar are found in Matthew (Matthew 19:13-30) and Mark (Mark 10:13-52).

1. Parable of the Persistent Widow (Luke 18:1-8):

- Discuss the parable of the persistent widow and its message about the importance of perseverance in prayer. What does this parable teach us about how we should approach prayer and our relationship with God?

- Reflect on the question Jesus poses at the end of the parable: "When the Son of Man comes, will he find faith on the earth?" How does this challenge us to cultivate a deep and persistent faith in our own lives?

2. **Parable of the Pharisee and the Tax Collector (Luke 18:9-14):**

- Examine the parable of the Pharisee and the tax collector, focusing on the contrast between their attitudes and approaches to prayer. What does this parable teach us about humility and self-righteousness in our relationship with God?

- Consider Jesus' statement, "For all those who exalt themselves will be humbled, and those who humble themselves will be exalted." How does this teaching challenge us to examine our own attitudes and actions in light of God's values?

3. **Jesus Blesses the Children (Luke 18:15-17):**

- Discuss Jesus' interaction with the children and His teaching that we must receive the Kingdom of God like a little child. What qualities of children might Jesus be emphasizing here, and how can we apply these qualities to our own faith journey?

4. **The Rich Young Ruler (Luke 18:18-30):**

- Explore the story of the rich young ruler who asks Jesus what he must do to inherit eternal life. What does Jesus' response and the ruler's reaction reveal about the challenge of wealth and the priorities of the Kingdom of God?

- Reflect on Jesus' statement that "it is easier for a camel to go through the eye of a needle than for someone who is rich to enter the Kingdom of God." How does this teaching call us to reevaluate our own priorities and reliance on material possessions?

5. **Jesus Foretells His Death and Resurrection (Luke 18:31-34):**

- Discuss Jesus' prediction of His death and resurrection and the disciples' lack of understanding. What does this reveal about the nature of Jesus' mission and the expectations of His followers at the time?

- Reflect on the significance of Jesus' willingness to suffer and die for humanity. How does this deepen our understanding of His love and sacrifice for us?

6. **Jesus Heals a Blind Beggar (Luke 18:35-43):**

- Examine the story of Jesus healing the blind beggar, focusing on the man's faith and persistence in calling out to Jesus. What can we learn from this man's example about the importance of faith and persistence in our own lives?

- Consider the response of the crowd when they witnessed the miracle. How does this event contribute to the growing awareness of Jesus' identity and mission?

Reflection and Discussion:

- How does Luke Chapter 18 challenge and inspire you to grow in your prayer life, humility, understanding of the role of wealth, and appreciation of Jesus' sacrifice in your relationship with God?

- What specific teachings or principles from Luke Chapter 18 can you apply to your own life to grow in your relationship with God and others?

Conclusion: As you reflect on Luke Chapter 18, seek to apply the insights and principles to your own faith and spiritual growth. Use

this study guide to facilitate discussion, personal reflection, and spiritual growth as you delve into the themes of prayer, humility, the challenge of wealth, and Jesus' foretelling of His death and resurrection. May your engagement with Luke Chapter 18 deepen your understanding of God's Word and strengthen your relationship with God and others.

Luke Chapter 19

Introduction:

- Summary: Jesus encounters Zacchaeus, a wealthy tax collector, who repents and receives Jesus with joy. Jesus tells the Parable of the Ten Minas, emphasizing the importance of using one's resources and opportunities wisely for the Kingdom of God. Jesus enters Jerusalem triumphantly, fulfilling prophecy, and weeps over the city's impending judgment. He cleanses the temple, driving out the money changers, and teaches daily in the temple, while the religious leaders plot against Him.

- Background: This chapter features the story of Zacchaeus, a powerful example of repentance and transformation, and the Parable of the Ten Minas, which underscores responsible stewardship. The chapter also describes Jesus' triumphal entry into Jerusalem and His cleansing of the temple, both of which foreshadow the climactic events of His ministry.

- Parallel references: The triumphal entry and the cleansing of the temple are found in Matthew (Matthew 21:1-17), Mark (Mark 11:1-19), and John (John 12:12-19, 2:13-22). The story of Zacchaeus and the Parable of the Ten Minas are unique to the Gospel of Luke.

1. Zacchaeus the Tax Collector (Luke 19:1-10):

- Discuss the encounter between Jesus and Zacchaeus, a tax collector. What does this story teach us about the power of Jesus to transform lives and the importance of embracing His grace?

83

- Reflect on the significance of Jesus seeking out and accepting someone like Zacchaeus, who was despised by society. How does this challenge our own attitudes towards those who may be considered "outcasts" in our communities?

2. **The Parable of the Ten Minas (Luke 19:11-27):**

- Analyze the Parable of the Ten Minas, focusing on the themes of stewardship, responsibility, and faithfulness. What does this parable teach us about how we should use the gifts and resources God has entrusted to us?

- Consider the implications of this parable for our own lives. How can we be faithful stewards of what God has given us and prepare for His return?

3. **Jesus' Triumphal Entry into Jerusalem (Luke 19:28-44):**

- Examine the events surrounding Jesus' triumphal entry into Jerusalem. What do these events reveal about Jesus' identity as the Messiah, and how do they fulfill Old Testament prophecies?

- Reflect on the people's response to Jesus' entry and their failure to recognize the significance of the moment. What lessons can we learn from this about recognizing and embracing Jesus as our Savior and King?

4. **Jesus Cleanses the Temple (Luke 19:45-48):**

- Discuss Jesus' actions in cleansing the Temple, driving out those who were buying and selling. What does this event teach us about Jesus' authority and His concern for the sanctity of God's house?

- Reflect on the response of the religious leaders to Jesus' actions and teachings in the Temple. How does this illustrate the ongoing conflict between Jesus and the religious authorities throughout His ministry?

Reflection and Discussion:

- How does Luke Chapter 19 challenge and inspire you to embrace Jesus' transformative grace, practice faithful stewardship, recognize Jesus as the Messiah, and respect His authority?
- What specific teachings or principles from Luke Chapter 19 can you apply to your own life to grow in your relationship with God and others?

Conclusion: As you reflect on Luke Chapter 19, seek to apply the insights and principles to your own faith and spiritual growth. Use this study guide to facilitate discussion, personal reflection, and spiritual growth as you delve into the themes of transformation, stewardship, recognition of Jesus as the Messiah, and Jesus' authority. May your engagement with Luke Chapter 19 deepen your understanding of God's Word and strengthen your relationship with God and others.

Luke Chapter 20

Introduction:

- Summary: The religious leaders question Jesus' authority, and He responds with the Parable of the Tenants, which serves as an indictment against them for rejecting God's messengers, including Jesus Himself. They try to trap Jesus with questions about paying taxes to Caesar and the resurrection, but Jesus skillfully evades their traps and exposes their hypocrisy. Jesus warns against the scribes and their ostentatious displays of piety.

- Background: This chapter highlights the ongoing conflict between Jesus and the religious authorities. The Parable of the Tenants serves as a prophetic warning about their rejection of Jesus and the consequences that would follow. Jesus' teachings emphasize His wisdom and authority, as well as the dangers of religious hypocrisy.

- Parallel references: The Parable of the Tenants, the question about paying taxes to Caesar, the question about the resurrection, and the warning against the scribes are found in Matthew (Matthew 21:33-46, 22:15-46, 23:1-36) and Mark (Mark 12:1-44).

1. Authority of Jesus Questioned (Luke 20:1-8):

- Examine the religious leaders' questioning of Jesus' authority and His response. What does this exchange teach us about Jesus' wisdom and His ability to expose the motives of His opponents?

- Consider the implications of this exchange for our own understanding of Jesus' authority and the importance of submitting to His teachings and guidance.

2. **Parable of the Wicked Tenants (Luke 20:9-19):**

- Discuss the Parable of the Wicked Tenants, focusing on the themes of rejection, judgment, and the consequences of disobedience. What does this parable teach us about the response of the religious leaders to Jesus and the consequences of rejecting Him?

- Reflect on the fulfillment of this parable in Jesus' crucifixion and the ultimate victory of God's plan. How does this parable provide hope for those who follow Jesus?

3. **Paying Taxes to Caesar (Luke 20:20-26):**

- Discuss Jesus' response to the question about paying taxes to Caesar. What does His answer teach us about the relationship between our earthly responsibilities and our commitment to God?

- Consider the implications of Jesus' teaching on taxes for our own understanding of civic responsibilities and our ultimate allegiance to God.

4. **Teaching on Marriage and Resurrection (Luke 20:27-40):**

- Analyze Jesus' teaching on marriage and resurrection in response to the Sadducees' question. What does this teaching reveal about the nature of the resurrection and eternal life in God's kingdom?

- Reflect on the importance of understanding the Scriptures and the power of God in our own lives. How can we apply

Jesus' teaching on the resurrection to our faith and hope in God's promises?

5. Question about the Messiah (Luke 20:41-44):

- Examine Jesus' question to the religious leaders about the identity of the Messiah. What does this question reveal about Jesus' understanding of His own identity and the fulfillment of Old Testament prophecies?

- Reflect on the significance of Jesus as both David's son and David's Lord. How does this understanding of Jesus' identity deepen our appreciation for His role as the Messiah?

6. Jesus Denounces the Scribes (Luke 20:45-47):

- Discuss Jesus' denunciation of the scribes and their hypocritical behavior. What does this condemnation teach us about the dangers of religious hypocrisy and the importance of genuine faith and humility?

- Reflect on how Jesus' teaching about the scribes can help us examine our own motives and behavior to ensure that we are living authentically in our faith.

Reflection and Discussion:

- How does Luke Chapter 20 challenge and inspire you to recognize Jesus' authority, understand His teachings, and embrace His wisdom?
- What specific teachings or principles from Luke Chapter 20 can you apply to your own life to grow in your relationship with God and others?

Conclusion: As you reflect on Luke Chapter 20, seek to apply the insights and principles to your own faith and spiritual growth. Use this study guide to facilitate discussion, personal reflection, and spiritual growth as we can see how Jesus, in His final days, continued to teach and challenge the religious leaders of His time. His authority was questioned, yet He masterfully turned the tables on those trying to trap Him with their questions. Jesus not only demonstrated wisdom but also revealed the true nature of His kingdom and His mission on earth.

Luke Chapter 21

Introduction:

- Summary: Jesus praises a poor widow for her sacrificial offering at the temple. He then predicts the destruction of the temple and Jerusalem, along with signs of the end times, including false messiahs, wars, natural disasters, and persecution. Jesus encourages His followers to be watchful and prayerful, standing firm in their faith until His return.

- Background: This chapter deals with Jesus' teachings on the end times and the need for vigilance and faithfulness. The prediction of the temple's destruction serves as a stark reminder of the consequences of rejecting Jesus and His message.

- Parallel references: The widow's offering and Jesus' predictions about the end times are found in Matthew (Matthew 24:1-44) and Mark (Mark 13:1-37).

1. The Widow's Offering (Luke 21:1-4):

- Discuss the widow's offering and Jesus' commendation of her. What does this event teach us about the nature of true generosity and the value of sacrificial giving?

- Reflect on the implications of the widow's offering for our own understanding of stewardship and the importance of giving from a heart of faith and devotion.

2. Jesus Foretells the Destruction of the Temple (Luke 21:5-6):

- Examine Jesus' prediction of the temple's destruction in response to the disciples' admiration of the temple's beauty. What does this prophecy teach us about the temporary nature of earthly institutions and the importance of focusing on eternal realities?

- Consider the fulfillment of Jesus' prophecy in the destruction of the temple in 70 AD. How does this event validate Jesus' authority and the truth of His teachings?

3. **Signs of the End Times (Luke 21:7-24):**

- Analyze Jesus' teaching on the signs of the end times, including wars, natural disasters, persecution, and the desolation of Jerusalem. What do these signs reveal about the unfolding of God's plan and the approach of the end of the age?

- Reflect on the importance of discerning the signs of the times and understanding their significance in light of God's purposes and promises.

4. **The Coming of the Son of Man (Luke 21:25-28):**

- Discuss Jesus' description of the coming of the Son of Man and the cosmic signs that will accompany His return. What does this teaching reveal about the ultimate triumph of God's kingdom and the hope of all who trust in Jesus?

- Reflect on the implications of Jesus' teaching on the coming of the Son of Man for our own lives, including the importance of living with hope and expectancy as we await His return.

5. **The Lesson of the Fig Tree and the Importance of Watchfulness (Luke 21:29-36):**

- Examine Jesus' lesson of the fig tree and His call to watchfulness in the face of the end times. What does this teaching teach us about the importance of discernment and preparedness as we await Jesus' return?

- Reflect on the implications of Jesus' teaching on watchfulness for our own spiritual lives, including the importance of prayer, vigilance, and living with a sense of urgency in light of Jesus' imminent return.

6. Jesus' Teaching in the Temple (Luke 21:37-38):

- Discuss Jesus' daily teaching in the temple and the eagerness of the people to hear Him. What does this passage reveal about Jesus' commitment to teaching and the receptiveness of the people to His message?

- Reflect on the importance of seeking out and engaging with Jesus' teachings in our own lives, and consider how we can cultivate a similar eagerness to learn and grow in our faith.

Reflection and Discussion:

- How does Luke Chapter 21 challenge and inspire you to practice sacrificial giving, discern the signs of the times, live with watchfulness and expectancy as we await Jesus' return, and engage with His teachings?
- What specific teachings or principles from Luke Chapter 21 can you apply to your own life to grow in faith, deepen your relationship with Jesus, and live with a greater sense of purpose and urgency?

Conclusion: As you reflect on Luke Chapter 21, take time to consider the lessons and insights found in this loaded chapter. Which of the topics presented have had the most impact on you? May this study guide inspire you to grow in your faith, live with watchfulness and expectancy, and embrace the transformative power of Jesus' teachings in your life.

Luke Chapter 22

Introduction:

- Summary: The religious leaders plot to kill Jesus, and Judas agrees to betray Him. Jesus celebrates the Last Supper with His disciples, instituting the Lord's Supper as a memorial of His death and establishing the new covenant in His blood. He predicts Peter's denial and teaches about true greatness and service. Jesus prays in the Garden of Gethsemane, agonizing over His impending suffering but submitting to the Father's will. He is betrayed by Judas, arrested, and brought before the religious leaders, who mock and beat Him. Peter denies Jesus three times, just as Jesus had predicted.

- Background: This chapter describes the events leading up to Jesus' crucifixion, including the Last Supper, His prayer in Gethsemane, and His arrest. The Last Supper is a pivotal moment in which Jesus institutes the new covenant and emphasizes the significance of His sacrificial death.

- Parallel references: The Last Supper, Jesus' prayer in Gethsemane, His arrest, and Peter's denial are found in Matthew (Matthew 26:17-75), Mark (Mark 14:12-72), and John (John 13:1-30, 18:1-27).

1. The Plot to Kill Jesus and Judas' Betrayal (Luke 22:1-6):

- Discuss the religious leaders' plot to kill Jesus and the role Judas plays in this plan. What does this reveal about the motivations and hearts of those involved?

- Reflect on the consequences of Judas' betrayal and the impact it has on Jesus' final days. What can we learn from

Judas' choices about the importance of discernment and remaining faithful to Jesus?

2. **The Last Supper (Luke 22:7-23):**

- Examine the events of the Last Supper and Jesus' institution of the Lord's Supper. What is the significance of this meal in Jesus' ministry and the life of the early church?

- Consider Jesus' words about the bread and the wine representing His body and blood. How do these symbols help us remember Jesus' sacrifice and the new covenant He established through His death?

3. **Jesus Teaches on Servant Leadership and the Future (Luke 22:24-38):**

- Discuss Jesus' teaching on servant leadership in response to the disciples' dispute about greatness. What principles of leadership does Jesus emphasize, and how do they differ from worldly ideas about power and authority?

- Reflect on Jesus' own example of servant leadership throughout His ministry. How can you apply these principles to your own life, relationships, and areas of influence?

- Examine Jesus' instructions to the disciples in verses 35-38. How do these teachings prepare the disciples for future challenges and the mission Jesus has for them?

4. **Jesus Predicts Peter's Denial (Luke 22:31-34):**

- Examine Jesus' prediction of Peter's denial and Peter's response. What can we learn from Peter's overconfidence and eventual failure?

- Consider the role of prayer and dependence on God in overcoming temptation and standing firm in our faith. How can you cultivate a prayerful and humble attitude in the face of challenges and temptations?

5. **Jesus Prays in the Garden of Gethsemane (Luke 22:39-46):**

- Discuss Jesus' time of prayer and anguish in the Garden of Gethsemane. What does this reveal about Jesus' humanity and His deep connection to the Father?

- Reflect on Jesus' prayer, "not my will, but yours be done." How does this example of submission and trust in God challenge and inspire you in your own prayer life and relationship with God?

6. **Jesus' Arrest, Peter's Denial, and Jesus' Trials (Luke 22:47-71):**

- Examine the events surrounding Jesus' arrest and Peter's denial. How do these events fulfill Jesus' earlier predictions?

- Consider the lessons we can learn from Peter's denial and his eventual restoration. How can we grow in faithfulness and perseverance, even when we experience failure or weakness in our walk with Jesus?

- Discuss Jesus' trials before the religious leaders in verses 63-71. What do these trials reveal about the false accusations against Jesus and the determination of the religious leaders to condemn Him?

Reflection and Discussion:

- How does Luke Chapter 22 challenge and inspire you to grow in your understanding of Jesus' sacrifice, the importance of servant leadership, and the role of prayer and dependence on God in your spiritual life?

- What specific teachings or principles from Luke Chapter 22 can you apply to your own life to grow in your relationship with God and others?

Conclusion: As you reflect on Luke Chapter 22, seek to apply the insights and principles to your own life, deepening your understanding of Jesus' sacrifice, His teachings on servant leadership, and the power of prayer. Recognize the significance of Jesus' trials and the fulfillment of His predictions, and consider how these events can shape your own faith and walk with God. Be encouraged to persevere, even in the face of failure or weakness, as you remember Peter's story and the grace that Jesus extends to all who follow Him.

Luke Chapter 23

Introduction:

- Summary: Jesus is brought before Pilate and then Herod Antipas, who both find Him innocent but ultimately yield to the pressure from the religious leaders and the crowd. Jesus is crucified between two criminals, and one of them repents and receives Jesus' promise of salvation. Jesus dies, and the temple veil is torn, symbolizing the end of the old covenant and the access to God provided through Jesus' sacrifice. He is buried in a tomb provided by Joseph of Arimathea, a member of the Jewish council who had not agreed with the decision to crucify Jesus.

- Background: This chapter details the crucifixion of Jesus, the central event of Christianity, which demonstrates God's love and the sacrifice required for the forgiveness of sins. The tearing of the temple veil signifies a new era in which all people can have direct access to God through Jesus' atoning death.

- Parallel references: Jesus' trial, crucifixion, death, and burial are found in Matthew (Matthew 27:1-66), Mark (Mark 15:1-47), and John (John 18:28-19:42).

1. Jesus' Trial before Pilate and Herod (Luke 23:1-25):

- Examine the accusations against Jesus and Pilate's initial verdict. How does Pilate's response to the religious leaders reveal his struggle with the decision to crucify Jesus?

- Discuss Jesus' interaction with Herod and the significance of Herod's involvement in Jesus' trial.

2. The Crucifixion (Luke 23:26-43):

- Reflect on Jesus' words to the women of Jerusalem who mourned for Him. What do these words reveal about Jesus' compassion and the impending judgment on Jerusalem?

- Analyze the interactions between Jesus and the two criminals crucified with Him. How do their responses to Jesus differ, and what can we learn from their reactions to Jesus in the face of death?

3. The Death of Jesus and the Centurion's Response (Luke 23:44-49):

- Discuss the supernatural events that occurred at Jesus' death, including the darkness and the tearing of the temple curtain. What is the significance of these events in the context of Jesus' crucifixion?

- Reflect on the response of the Roman centurion and the onlookers at Jesus' crucifixion. What do their reactions reveal about their understanding of Jesus and the events that took place?

4. Jesus' Burial (Luke 23:50-56):

- Examine the role of Joseph of Arimathea in Jesus' burial. How does his involvement in Jesus' burial demonstrate his faith and devotion?

- Consider the actions of the women who followed Jesus and observed His burial. What can we learn from their example of faithfulness and devotion to Jesus?

Reflection and Discussion:

- How does Luke Chapter 23 challenge and inspire you to deepen your understanding of Jesus' sacrifice and the significance of His crucifixion?

- What specific teachings or principles from Luke Chapter 23 can you apply to your own life to grow in your relationship with God and others?

Conclusion: As you reflect on Luke Chapter 23, seek to apply the insights and principles to your own life, deepening your understanding of Jesus' sacrifice, His trial, and crucifixion. Recognize the injustice Jesus faced and the ultimate redemption He provided through His death on the cross. Be encouraged by the faith and devotion of the individuals who followed Jesus and consider how their examples can inspire your own walk with God.

Introduction:

- Summary: On the first day of the week, women who had followed Jesus find His tomb empty and are told by angels that He has risen from the dead. The women report the news to the disciples, but their story is initially met with disbelief. Jesus appears to two disciples on the road to Emmaus, explaining how the Scriptures pointed to His death and resurrection. They recognize Him when He breaks bread with them. Jesus then appears to the rest of the disciples, proving His resurrection and opening their minds to understand the Scriptures. He commissions them to preach the Gospel and promises to send the Holy Spirit. Jesus leads them to the vicinity of Bethany, blesses them, and ascends into heaven.

- Background: The final chapter of the Gospel of Luke focuses on the resurrection of Jesus and His post-resurrection appearances, affirming the reality of His victory over death and the fulfillment of the Scriptures. Jesus' commission to the disciples and His ascension mark the end of His earthly ministry and the beginning of the Church's mission to spread the Gospel to all nations.

- Parallel references: The resurrection, Jesus' appearances to the disciples, and His ascension are found in Matthew (Matthew 28:1-20), Mark (Mark 16:1-20), and John (John 20:1-21:25). The story of the two disciples on the road to Emmaus is unique to the Gospel of Luke.

1. **The Empty Tomb and the Angels' Message (Luke 24:1-12):**

- Examine the women's discovery of the empty tomb and the angels' message about Jesus' resurrection. How do the women's reactions and their report to the disciples highlight the significance of the resurrection?

- Discuss the response of the disciples to the women's account. What does their initial skepticism reveal about the challenges of accepting Jesus' resurrection?

2. **Jesus Appears on the Road to Emmaus (Luke 24:13-35):**

- Reflect on the conversation between Jesus and the two disciples on the road to Emmaus. How does Jesus use the Old Testament scriptures to help the disciples understand the events of His crucifixion and resurrection?

- Analyze the disciples' recognition of Jesus and their decision to return to Jerusalem. What does their response to Jesus' revelation teach us about the transformative power of encountering the risen Savior?

3. **Jesus Appears to the Disciples in Jerusalem (Luke 24:36-49):**

- Discuss Jesus' appearance to the disciples in Jerusalem and His reassurance of His resurrection. How does Jesus provide evidence of His physical resurrection, and why is this important for the disciples' faith?

- Reflect on Jesus' explanation of how His death and resurrection fulfill Old Testament prophecies. How does this help the disciples understand the purpose and significance of Jesus' mission?

4. **The Great Commission and the Ascension (Luke 24:50-53):**

- Examine Jesus' final instructions to the disciples, known as the Great Commission. Compare with Matthew 28:18-20 where a much fuller description of the Commission is given. What are the key elements of this commission, and how does it shape the mission of the early church and believers today?

- Discuss Jesus' ascension into heaven and the disciples' response. How does their worship and joy reveal their understanding and acceptance of Jesus' resurrection and divine mission?

Reflection and Discussion:

- How does Luke Chapter 24 challenge and inspire you to deepen your faith in the resurrection of Jesus and the fulfillment of Old Testament prophecies?

- What specific teachings or principles from Luke Chapter 24 can you apply to your own life to grow in your relationship with God and others?

Conclusion: As you reflect on Luke Chapter 24, seek to apply the insights and principles to your own life, deepening your understanding of Jesus' resurrection and His fulfillment of Old Testament prophecies. Be inspired by the faith and devotion of the disciples as they encountered the risen Savior and carried out His Great Commission. May your engagement with Luke Chapter 24 strengthen your faith and encourage you to share the good news of Jesus with others.

Conclusion

As we conclude this Gospel of Luke Chapter-by-Chapter Bible Study Guide, we want to express our heartfelt gratitude to each one of you who has invested your time, energy, and resources into deepening your understanding of God's Word. Your commitment to spiritual growth and your pursuit of a closer relationship with Jesus are truly commendable.

We hope that this study guide has been a valuable tool in your journey of faith, helping you to delve deeper into the life and teachings of Jesus as revealed in the Gospel of Luke. Our prayer is that the insights, questions, and reflections provided in this guide have challenged you to apply the truths of Scripture to your daily life and have drawn you closer to the heart of God.

As you continue to seek God through the study of His Word, we invite you to explore more resources always available at **studychapterbychapter.com**. Our website offers an extensive range of Bible study guides in this series, designed to help you engage with Scripture in a meaningful and transformative way. Whether you are studying individually or in a small group setting, we are confident that these study guides will enrich your understanding of the Bible and encourage you in your walk with Christ.

Once again, thank you for your dedication to studying the Gospel of Luke and for allowing us to be a part of your spiritual journey. May God bless you abundantly as you continue to seek Him through the study of His Word and may the Holy Spirit guide and empower you to live as a faithful disciple of Jesus Christ.

In His service,

Barry L. Davis

Made in the USA
Las Vegas, NV
11 February 2025

17888093R00059